PRAISE FOR
Waiting for the Thaw

A MUST READ, *Waiting for the Thaw*: A powerful, fairytale-like story of love, family, business growth, and achievement in a changing pre and post-pandemic world. The challenges of the unknown and unexpected are magnified with the events of January 16, 2019.

The story highlights a young woman coming into her own as a dynamic, proficient businesswoman at the side of her husband and business partner. She displays an uncanny and expert understanding of business principles, knowledge, and skills, enabling her to continue the growth and success of their family business endeavors.

Her ongoing positive impact on family, friends, employees, and business partners is unparalleled, especially because she is struggling through the fog of debilitating grief, sorrow, and loss.

Edie Waddell,
CEO/President/Co-Founder
Landmark Custom Builder & Remodeling, LLC

WAITING
FOR THE
THAW

The Journey,
the Unspeakable Loss,
and the Transformation

Patricia Ann

**MADE FOR
SUCCESS**

Made for Success Publishing
P.O. Box 1775 Issaquah, WA 98027
www.MadeForSuccess.com

Distributed by Blackstone Publishing

First Printing

Library of Congress Cataloging-in-Publication data

Ann, Patricia
    Waiting for the Thaw: The Journey, the Unspeakable Loss,
    and the Transformation
        p. cm.

LCCN: 2024934381
ISBN: 978-1-64146-870-1 *(Paperback)*
ISBN: 978-1-64146-871-8 *(eBook)*
ISBN: 978-1-64146-872-5 *(Audiobook)*

Printed in the United States of America

For further information, contact Made for Success Publishing
+1(425) 526-6480 or email service@madeforsuccess.net

*Dedicated to the two girls who complete my life,
my daughters Nicole and Christine.
Love forever and always,
Mom*

"Be thankful for every new challenge,
each will give you more strength, wisdom,
and character."

—Kristen Butler

Chapter 1

HISTORY IN THE MAKING

WHEN I GRADUATED high school, I wasn't really interested in the whole college idea. I wanted to get right into the "working world" and begin experiencing life.

My amazing mom never worked until her later years. She dedicated and devoted her life to raising her five children. My four brothers and I never lacked the basics, but our family's modest means meant there wasn't much available in college funds. There really was no pressure from our parents to go to college.

Shortly after graduation, I landed a full-time job at Xerox. The position was for a security guard. It sounded pretty cool; the only disappointing thing was I would not be required to carry a gun. Not that I had a gun permit, mind you, but at the time, my ultimate goal in my life was to be an FBI agent. The job was for the late shift, and it required me to sit at a desk all night for eight long hours. The only exception was during the hourly clock checks. These hourly clocks were in the manufacturing area of Xerox.

I wouldn't say I was overly thrilled with this part of my job. Brave would not be a word I would choose to describe myself, but doing the nightly tour took a lot of bravery. Having to punch in at each checkpoint in this dimly lit plant advanced my athletic ability. I think if there had ever been a contest for who completed this task the fastest, I would have won. I sprinted through the dark hallways of the manufacturing plant, barely noticing the artwork on all the lockers and walls, you know, nude pictures of women posing in every position imaginable. Not exactly a comfortable and safe environment. Despite these quirks, I was only eighteen, and for the first time, I was receiving a check for over one hundred eighty dollars. I began to think I was starting to "make it."

Even though the pay was rewarding, the job itself consisted of a lot of alone time. The job made me reflect daily, and more importantly, it made me want to go out and mingle with civilization.

My close friends and I liked to frequent a bar called The Varsity Inn. The Varsity Inn was located on Scottsville Road in Rochester, New York, which is out in no man's land. It was surrounded by an unpaved parking lot and miles of nothing. Inside, there were two large dance floors and a packed thirty-foot bar. Tables were nestled around the dance floors, including in some hidden corners, where patrons could have private moments. The dance floors were usually sticky from spilled drinks, and they were always crowded. We were constantly out there dancing. We felt we were the best dancers on that sticky dance floor, and if nothing else, that was the place to be.

So, on the night of my eighteenth birthday, I picked up my closest girlfriends, Bonny, Barb, and Dawn. I was driving an orange Mach 1, a wildly unpredictable choice of vehicle for me. My parents bought this car for my high school graduation. It was a cool car, but it was a bit out of my comfort zone, and I can't pinpoint the reason I was attracted to it. But that didn't matter. All that mattered on this particular night was having a blast.

There we were, after a five-dollar cover charge, at The Varsity Inn. It was the hottest bar in town. Keep in mind, I didn't say it was the cleanest, or that it had the best music, or even that it had great drinks, but this hot spot seemed to draw attention anyway. As usual, the thirty-foot bar was three deep with people waiting impatiently for drinks. Shoulder to shoulder, they came from all walks of life: college students, bikers, and 9-to-5 workers.

I was excited to use my real ID, not the fake one I'd been using that showed me a year older than I actually was. Once we got into the bar, we had to work our way through the crowd to grab a watered-down drink, and then we descended on our hunt for a table. Life couldn't get any better than this! We found a table in the middle of the room located right next to the two dance floors. The perfect spot. Then, over the loudspeaker, we heard an announcement. "The VI is hosting a wet T-shirt contest. All interested contestants, go sign up!"

I thought to myself, *A WHAT?*

There was a rush of girls of all ages signing up to be the perfect contestant. They looked like they couldn't wait to expose themselves on stage in a flimsy, soaking-wet T-shirt. Classy, right? That was the VI. Oh, and it gets better! As we were sitting back in our chairs, being judges for each girl, a biker yelled out, "Take it off!"

As you can imagine, in situations like this, there is always a taker. Before we knew it, one of the contestants took off her very wet T-shirt for all to see. From that moment on, all hell broke loose. The next thing I knew, my girlfriends and I were watching as beer flew in midair, guys tried to get up on stage, and fists were flying. You know, the behavior you would expect of young adults.

Oh yes, by the way, she did win the contest. But her moment of glory was diminished by all the fights happening around us. Many were thrown out of the bar that night. "The good ole days," and what a night it was turning out to be.

Once the bar settled again, I decided to tell my friends about an encounter I'd had with one of the bouncers the last time we were at this place. Just as I was starting to talk about it, he passed our table, looking in the other direction. Quietly, I told my friends about the "come on" from this bouncer and pointed him out. My best friend, Bonny, said, "You should have gone out with him. He has a nice ass."

I immediately thought to myself, *Who knew I was supposed to be looking at that?* After a little more thought, I wondered if maybe I had missed an opportunity. To move forward with this inclination, I had to prove to myself that he was still interested without being embarrassed if he wasn't. I devised a plan to confirm whether or not he was of the same mindset as last time, and once executed, I would decide what to do next. I made a plan to walk myself to the bathroom, which is where he was standing, doing that "bouncer" thing. If he reached out and grabbed my arm or initiated a conversation, that would be the confirmation I needed. So here goes . . . and YES, he grabbed my arm, pulled me into him, and repeated the question he had asked before. In fact, as I think back, it wasn't a question; it was a statement. He said, "I think you should go out with me."

"I think you should go out with me." History in the making.

I thought that was a pretty arrogant statement, filled with confidence. Was it confidence, or maybe just a way not to get too bruised if I responded "no way"?

I responded, "Really, why?"

Quickly, he replied, "You look like Barbara Streisand."

That was all I had to hear; I wasn't fond of her or her look. I laughed out loud and continued to proceed to the lady's bathroom. I realized I didn't even get his name, and I was curious. Despite his answer, he'd caught my attention. He was tall, dark, and handsome. I know, a cliché, right? He had a lot of dark hair and a mischievous smile.

While I was in the bathroom, so many thoughts ran through my head. My final thought about this guy was he really didn't fit in at The Varsity Inn. He seemed different. A difference that made me want to take a chance.

Exiting the bathroom, I approached him and said, "It would be nice if I knew your name."

He asked the barmaid for a piece of paper—keep in mind, we didn't have cell phones—and he signed his name for me, or so I thought. As I turned the paper over to see his name, I saw that he'd put a large *X*. I looked at him, and he smiled and laughed. I thought, *What the hell have I gotten myself into?*

The way the first date went, you would have thought this was never going to work. One hour late, no call, he just rolled up in my parents' driveway. That is just not okay!

When Don came to the door, I simply asked without too much attitude, "Why so late?"

His response would've sent a seasoned dating girl off the deep end.

"I had to clean my car," he replied as he looked over his shoulder at his Corvette.

I thought to myself, *Well, a clean car is better than a dirty one.*

I introduced Don to my mom, and we quickly got into his Corvette and drove off. I remember the look on my mom's face. It was not a "have a good time, honey" look; it was more like "What the hell is going on here?" Don was an older guy with a sports car and no regard for time. Here we go!

We drove to the Vineyard, an Italian restaurant that served food buffet style. Coming from a family of seven, which included four brothers and myself, I could eat. As a matter of fact, I could pretty much eat like my brothers and didn't think twice about it. The look on Don's face when I walked up to the buffet a second time was funny. He commented, "It's nice to see a girl who actually eats." I immediately became self-conscious and began to wonder if I had just done something wrong. I gave him the benefit of the doubt and decided it was a compliment and I'd just taken it the wrong way. Let's face it: first dates are always awkward because we don't know anything about the other person. There were no cell phones or social media to dig up stuff about people.

After dinner, we set off for a Saint John Fischer football game. When Don told me we were going there, I just nodded, but in my head, I thought, *You have got to be kidding me!*

Football, seriously? This is your idea of a first date? Keep in mind, I have four brothers, and my life was consumed with sports, ugh! I diligently refrained from making any negative comments and just smiled. But as I was smiling, I was asking myself, *Who am I?*

I had always struggled with keeping my opinions to myself. I wasn't brought up like that, I guess, so to keep quiet was huge for me. As luck would have it, we left at half-time. As we were driving, he asked me if I knew where we were just as he strategically passed the Churchville sign.

I responded, "Churchville."

Then he asked me, "Do you know who lives in Churchville?"

I felt like I was in a game show, and I responded politely, "You do." Thinking to myself, *I'm eighteen, not five.* I just giggled to myself. The thought hit me at that point: he couldn't read me and didn't know how to relate to me yet. This made me relax, and then the conversation became easier, and in the end, the date was great. I discovered through our time together that his age didn't bother me; it actually piqued my curiosity, and I liked it.

We had it all. Don always said, "If we control our world, we will be okay."

On January 17, 2019, all the control we diligently built was lost forever. Now, what do I do? I feel as if the house has crumbled all around me, and I need to somehow dig myself out of the rubble and look for survivors.

To describe what a person goes through at this time is almost impossible. Your thoughts are not your own. Activity goes on all around you, but your mind is in complete shock.

Forty-one years of bliss. Loving, forgiving, honoring, supporting, and growing together. Don and I were usually on the same page about the important things, or what seemed to be important at that point in our lives. Don was confident in doing things his way, and I went along. The thoughts or opinions of others didn't affect us. In love, experiencing everything for the first time together, I was powerless to wish for more.

Now, my safe zone is the mausoleum where Don is located. There is no outside world, no "I'm so sorry for your loss" comments, and no "What are you going to do?" questions. It's the perfect hidden, quiet place for me to descend into the free fall I seem to be doing so much lately. I need peace; I need some type of peace.

"Never quit and you will never lose."

—Vince Lombardi

Chapter 2

TYING THE KNOT

DON WAS SEVEN years older than me, and he was divorced. That was not information we shared; it was our secret. I say secret, but when I decided that Don was the man I would end up with, I had to tell my mom.

I was extremely nervous, but I would never hide a detail about Don from my mom and dad. All our conversations were pretty much held at the dining room table, our only eating area, which was smack in the center of the house. The only thing I had to clearly plan out was the timing. I didn't want my nosy but caring brothers to participate in the conversation. I had no interest in their opinions. So, when it looked as if the coast was clear, I went for it.

When I started the conversation, my wise and intuitive mom conveniently finished it for me. I always believed my mom was psychic, and this conversation proved to me that she had an intuition that could not be ignored. She completed my sentence, stating, "He is divorced," and I said yes.

To better understand my upbringing, especially when it came to my mom, it's important to know that she never assumed or attacked. She had the most tactful way of getting her point across, and usually, by the end of the conversation, you agreed with her. She had this special ability to open your eyes to another perspective. I understood why she said things like, "Take your time," "Leave yourself open to other opportunities and other relationships," and "You're young and just graduated from high school; there's plenty of time to figure out what's real and what isn't."

But with this decision about Don, I stood firm, and I responded, "Mom, this is it for me. I just know."

When I got engaged at a later date, she did, however, attempt to talk me out of my decision, which was not an easy task. I felt so strongly about my feelings for Don. I just knew there was a connection I could not deny, and I did not have any interest in doing so. She even asked my older brother Anthony to talk with me, obviously in a more casual setting, and I told him, "Please, I know what I am doing."

Don's divorce was not an issue for me, and neither was the age difference. I knew they were just worried about me since I was pretty sheltered and only dated one boyfriend all through high school—and now this. I did understand their concern, and I knew it came from a place of love. This was foreign to all of us. I was feeling so attracted to this man, but he was outside of my family's comfort zone. As time heals all, my family eventually accepted the fact that Don was going to be part of all of our lives, and eventually, he was like one of the guys, playing football and competing with my brothers, giving them another body to bounce around. In my world, when you started dating someone new, my whole family tended to get involved on some level.

Dating on any level can be stressful. The "get to know each other" chapter is always interesting. Of course, I complicated this part of our dating period by leading Don to believe that I could actually cook. One night, I told him I was bringing dinner over, but in reality, the only thing I did was shop for a new outfit, get dressed, and make sure my makeup was done.

I have to admit that I always had pretty nice clothes. My mom was a shopper, and she definitely gave me that gene. She also never restricted me from wearing makeup at a younger age; she just guided me to the right amount, and I believe that was brilliant. There was no sneaking around with makeup in my school bag like a lot of the other girls at school. She understood that restricting was a recipe for failure and retaliation.

As the evening approached, my mom prepared the stuffed Cornish hens, vegetables, and salad, and she put them on a platter for me to carry over. I served it up as my own. I didn't even think twice or consider that this was probably a little deceitful. Don loved the Cornish hen and stuffing, commenting about what a good cook I was. I just responded, "Thank you so much." Then I thought to myself, *What did I just do? I really know better! Maybe it's time for me to watch my mom and actually take the time to learn what goes on in the kitchen.*

I can't say it was my proudest moment, but it still makes me laugh. Of course, it was pretty obvious when we did get married that I knew nothing about cooking, and I eventually decided to come clean.

Later on, Don asked me to help him organize his bills and send in the payments. During our dating stage, there were numerous times when his home phone was turned off due to nonpayment. He obviously wasn't very good with deadlines. So, I accepted the challenge. Considering I had never written a check for myself, I thought this might be a great time to learn.

Don was madly in love with cars, Corvettes to be exact. Shortly after I took responsibility for his payments, he purchased a new jet-black Corvette. About a week after he had possession of it, he got a phone call from his auto dealer telling him to return the car because there was no insurance on the vehicle.

Don, of course, responded, "That's impossible!" and immediately called his insurance agent.

The agent, a personal friend, said, "Come over so we can figure this out."

I tagged along and sat in the back of the office, but when the insurance company's name was mentioned, my eyes almost popped out of my head. I think I even spit out my gum. Fireman's Fund—*Oh, my God*—I took my new responsibility of paying Don's bills very seriously, but I had failed to actually open that bill because I thought it was a request for a donation to our local fire department! How would I know it was an actual insurance company requesting payment? Poor Don was put in the risk pool for driving with enormous costs. I, the coward that I was, kept this secret until after we were married.

We dated for one year, and we were married shortly after I turned nineteen. October 16th was our special day. Coming from a Catholic family, everyone usually got married in a church setting, which was now weighing on my mind. I had to somehow carry on the tradition in some manner to honor the older generation of my family that I held dear to my heart.

Don was divorced and never completed the declaration of nullity through the church, which meant no catholic church would marry us. Don's firm belief and natural instinct was to find a solution that would make everyone happy, or at least have no one suspect the difference. After doing some research, we found that the Episcopalian church service for marriage was extremely similar to a Catholic one. What a glorious day; now our families' elderly wouldn't even notice that it wasn't a Catholic service. In my heart of hearts, this did not faze me. I always believed that if it was true in my heart and Don's, then it would be accepted by God. I never really fully bought into all the rules of the Catholic religion.

The morning of our special day, the doorbell rang, and my dad answered it. It was a delivery of twelve beautiful long-stem red roses. Always a romantic, it overwhelmed me with anticipation to get this day underway and become Mrs. Patricia Salamone.

In all aspects, I was totally Don's. Mind, body, and soul. With me, he was kind, tender, patient, and gentle. His personality was on the serious side, and to my surprise, I actually found it very attractive.

He would take the time to explain everything to me, sometimes in way too much detail. Having the ability to multi-task came in handy at times when having conversations with Don. I could be carried off in my own thoughts and come back toward the end and still retain all that he'd said, at least most of the time!

Throughout the forty-one years that we were together, Don was a loving husband, devoted father, educator, and patient mentor to many. He was a caregiver, and he was good at it. His family was a good family. He was very private and invested little time in his extended family. His dad and mom were kind, although the warm fuzzies never really hit me with his mom. I actually knew she did not feel I was a good fit for her son, Donald. I was too young or whatever she cooked up in her mind. His mom's name was Josephine, and she was much older than my parents. Don was at the late end of his generation, and I was perfectly placed for my generation. His mom was just a few years shy of my grandparents' age. So, culturally speaking, her ideas might have been a little different from mine and my family's. She was old school and not very flexible. Shortly after we were married, she decided to pull me aside to inform me that she was done entertaining for the holidays, and it was my responsibility to do this. I was nineteen and blown away by this. I was just getting used to cooking a dinner that was actually edible. Needless to say, that is when Don said, "You handle your family, and I will handle mine." That was a great suggestion, and it paid off for many years: no hurt feelings and no interference.

In comparison, my family was close, and we were right in each other's faces, in a good way. We hid very few skeletons from each other, and if we thought we had secrets, trust me, we didn't. My parents, although they may have struggled with each other at times, never wavered from the lessons and beliefs they wanted to teach their five children. Work hard to support your family. Your kids always come first, and you give them enough unconditional love to last an eternity. That was the atmosphere I grew up in.

Being the only girl, born smack in the middle of my brothers, probably allowed me to get away with a lot more than my four brothers. Spoiled, yes, I was, and I loved it. I grew up with a fierce competitive edge because of them. I really had no other choice; I had to survive the brotherhood! I knew how to play sports from an early age, and I loved playing with plastic army men and my dolls. "Well-rounded" was a good way to describe me as a child. I was tough and didn't put up with much. I never felt that if you were male, you were any better. This was definitely from my mom. Everyone is their own individual and should be seen and respected as such. My mom possessed the kindest of hearts and was the glue of our family. She had the special ability to show us we were unique in our own way and that there was nothing more important than loving and respecting each other. That feeling resonated through all of us. Inserting our opinions or concerns was a common occurrence in our household; minding your own business was not something we considered. If you care and you see something you don't agree with, you make it your mission to voice your concern. That's what our family always did. Which, of course, included the somewhat frequent occurrence of snitching.

My family had a tradition of having Sunday dinners together, which continued even after we got married. I was the second Marsala to get married, and Don and

I always attended Sunday dinners. Sunday dinner was always sauce and pasta. The funny thing is that we had assigned seats at the dinner table. Unlike other families, we were allowed to have the TV on if there was a football game—no surprise there. Don's assigned seat was not his choice. He had no view of the football game and had to wait for my brothers to get married to move up to a better seat at the table. Another difference between Don and my family was that we inhaled our food, and he would actually eat at a slow pace. Most of the time, if not all of the time, he would be the only one left at the dinner table with my mom, enjoying whatever he wanted to watch on TV.

Since we had totally different family dynamics, the agreement Don and I made early in our relationship to deal with our respective families paid dividends and most likely saved us from a lot of arguments. We never wavered from this, and it seemed to protect the world we built with each other.

When we were first married, Don was involved in his family's business, building homes and snow plowing. This was when I realized he wanted to involve me in everything. I went out with him late at night plowing, going door to door asking people if they wanted their driveways plowed and, on occasion, asking if I could use their bathroom. It was very different back then.

We actually did quite well, with few equipment failures. When it came to home building, I would observe

Don during the sale, from contract to building, and then the collection of funds. I didn't realize at the time that this information would be useful at a later date.

Do we ever really know which situations are teaching us or preparing us for the future?

One thing I was learning about my new husband was that he could multi-task well. From my perspective, that seemed unusual for a man. He was also able to see and replicate; he was like a sponge with the ability to learn quickly and move on to something new. He had many interests, and with every new experience that he encountered, he would include me.

At the time, I didn't realize that I was learning so much. We were just spending time together. I appreciated the way he included me and took the time to explain things to me. He was a natural teacher. With me, he enjoyed talking, and we did a lot of that! He rarely complained. Instead, he would patiently work his way to where he needed or wanted to be. He was patient, the most patient person I had met so far in my nineteen years.

The absence of sound in my house is deafening. My mind never stops; it is my worst enemy. I need to find my shut-off button for my sanity. Forty-one years and now nothing, stripped of all that I knew. We built our heaven on earth,

only to be left empty. So many questions. Too many questions. I feel frozen! Frozen in life with no windows or doors.

I feel like I am stuck in an ice-blue castle, waiting for the thaw.

Will I make it out?

"Life is a series of tiny miracles, notice them."

—Roald Dahl

Chapter 3

BUNDLE OF JOY

I EVENTUALLY LEFT my employment at Xerox and moved over to Bowest, a mortgage company based out of California that was attempting to do business in New York. Forgoing my surreal FBI dreams, I entered Bowest's foreclosure department to work with homeowners who'd fallen upon hard times. It was difficult at times. Homeowners had to either go along with the recommended payment schedule to catch their mortgage up to date, or they lost their homes. Despite this, I enjoyed working at Bowest. I found delight in solving issues for homeowners affected by circumstances not necessarily caused by their own choices, but unfortunately, the writing was on the wall. You could feel that changes were coming, and the common belief among employees was that this California-based company would eventually stop doing business in New York State.

Don and I had been married for about one year, and everything was great. I depended on Don and his wisdom to help guide me, but I also needed to be the one ultimately making the final decision about my workplace. He introduced me to the concept of a pros and cons list. He had me list all the pros and cons of staying at Bowest. The list made my decision, and in the long run, it was the right one.

As the cons outweighed the pros, I decided to start the interview process, and as luck would have it, I was hired on the spot at Marine Midland Bank. I started as an adjuster located in the collections department. I really don't know how I gravitated in that direction, but there I was. My mindset from early on was, "I can do anything, or at least learn how to do it."

Competitiveness was in my blood. I started as a thirty-day adjuster and worked my way up to the lead adjuster with only one year of experience. I dealt with the unfortunate process of repossessions from customers who were over ninety days late on paying their auto loans. I surpassed all the guys in the department and pretty much did anything I wanted. I even did my nails at my desk and had to listen to the other employees complain about the smell of the nail polish remover. My supervisor would just shake his head, but he never reprimanded me. I won or was acknowledged for most of the contests that were in the department, and I pretty much called the shots in that little world.

At home, adjusting to married life was a breeze for us. We just blended well together. We shared everything and did almost everything together. Don wanted to include me in everything and expose me to all that he was doing, and we had fun doing it. We rarely argued, and when we did make up, it seemed like a fresh start with a new understanding of how to compromise and forgive.

Early on, we made a pact never to go to bed angry, and we worked diligently at this. It was not always accomplished, but our efforts always worked toward this goal. I had an easier time forgetting and moving on than Don. I used to call him the "three-day guy." If he was really upset over something, he would quietly drag it out for three days, and this drove me crazy. I remember telling him he was not perfect, and if I could forgive quickly, why couldn't he? He finally did acknowledge that this was something he had to improve on, but he struggled. I believe he couldn't hold out longer than three days because, well, let's just say he missed me.

Every day was an adventure of sorts. We traveled, we experienced things for the first time together, and I thought many times, *This can't get any better!* We were the romantic type of couple, always holding hands and always considering the thoughts and wishes of the other first. Alone time was our strength, and this in itself provided a confidence in each other that so few achieve in their marriages.

After four years of doing anything and everything we wanted, like traveling to Toronto every other weekend, I wanted and needed more. My maternal feelings were blossoming. I simply looked at Don one day, and I said, "It's time, I think, for us to have a baby and start a family."

He looked at me and simply replied, "Okay, want to start now?" That was that. No questions or concerns. He sort of blew me away. He was always a talker, and he usually analyzed every angle before committing to anything, but this reply calmly and playfully came rolling out of his mouth. I was definitely in love with all of him, and this was all I needed.

After we made the decision to have a baby, I became pregnant practically a second after we tried. I needed to give notice that I would not be returning to my luxurious job. I told Don I wanted to stay home and raise our child and be totally responsible for how they turned out. He, again, just simply agreed, and off we went in the direction that we felt was right. Don, being an entrepreneur, didn't seem to flinch at the thought of me quitting my job and becoming a stay-at-home mom. This, I knew, would put more stress on him, but if there were any problems at this point, he never involved me in them.

Our beautiful daughter Nicole was born within the year and brought us the immeasurable joy of being first-time parents. I had never heard of a colic baby, but Nicole introduced us to that. We discovered within the first few months that even though she was so tiny, she had a strong voice.

It was my belief that the baby had to be in our bedroom until she was at least one year old, but that didn't last beyond the second week after her birth. Her screams and cries, caused by distress from food intolerance or allergies, convinced me to move her into her own room where one of us could take care of her while the other attempted to get some rest.

Adjusting to the needs of the baby was difficult, but Don and I developed a schedule to relieve each other every four hours, and this was when I realized that Don was a caregiver; it was in his blood. He worked all day but insisted on having a night-shift feeding with Nicole. She eventually grew out of this stage but maintained her two o'clock feeding for a year and a half. She was so small and adorable at this time, always wanting to play or cuddle, so we both enjoyed getting up for that feeding. Nicole was a clone of her dad. She had his skin coloring and his black hair. They could never be denied as father and daughter. He was always at ease when handling her, even at the slight weight of five pounds, six ounces.

Meanwhile, I realized that being the wife of an entrepreneur meant, "Get ready, and I hope you enjoy rollercoaster rides." Let's face it: growth and decline in any business is stressful, whether you're prepared for it or not. Don was a private individual; he didn't share a lot in the beginning. He wouldn't burden our future with the present; it was just a roadblock to maneuver over. He would resolve things and move on. He often told me his brain was set up to just fix, fix the problem. I wasn't quite sure what he meant by that, but looking back, I believe his mindset was to resolve and restructure and not put too much emphasis on the current situation. Instead, he focused on the future and the results.

As I proceed to write these words as an exercise to help me heal, I realize how quiet my house is. My daughters have been clinging to me, and it is so appreciated. We need to strengthen each other.

I feel so bad for my daughters, losing their hero, their dad.

I know he meant the world to each of them.

This alone time is horrendous and difficult on every level.

The only noise in the house is the movie that is on the TV, Body Heat.

Now, memories of us watching this movie start to flood my thoughts, and again, the tears flow. I can't stop crying.

I am determined not to cry in front of my girls. I am aware I am not accomplishing this, but I am trying.

This has to be a nightmare. It can't be reality. It just can't be.

"It's never too late for anything."

—George Eliot

Chapter 4

OUR FAMILY ENDEAVORS

DON AND I enjoyed going out to dinner. We made this a ritual. In the early years, we ate out with a group that eventually dissolved as life took us in different directions. Despite the split, Don and I continued our habit of dining out because we enjoyed it, and one night, while we were having dinner at Ricks Prime Rib, an older couple sat next to us.

I say older, but keep in mind I was twenty-two years old, so forty would have seemed older. The nicely dressed woman looked at us and decided to give us some advice.

She said, "Marriage is a fifty-fifty proposition. Always remember that, and you will stay married forever."

I giggled and replied, "I agree."

The impact of those words resonates even deeper with me today. Marriage is fifty-fifty. Take responsibility for all that you can control, and make sure you share everything with your partner, and that means your heart and soul.

As life moved on, we lost our best friends to a bitter divorce, and then the other couples we were friends with also split up. It seemed to me that we had each other, and that was pretty much all we needed.

As disappointing as the news from our friends was, it never influenced Don and me. We were strong and experiencing everything together for the first time, enjoying the ups and downs.

When Nicole was about one-and-a-half years old, we both knew it was time to grow our family. Our second blessing was born eleven days late. She was small by today's standards, only six pounds, eleven ounces, and she was blessed with a head of dark curls. Don made it a point to select her name: Christine. Two wonderful daughters completed our lives and gave a new purpose to all of our future endeavors.

Life was full, and there was no stopping Don and I. He was a doer, and what I mean by that is he never could have been classified as a couch potato. We were involved in everything. Don's entrepreneurial spirit gave us a lifetime of memories and adventures. We were raising two daughters, and I was homebound, so I was up for anything.

The way Don would approach me with one of his ideas was pretty interesting. He would wrap the idea up as a pretty gift and present his best case. Whenever Don introduced a new idea to me, he always seemed to know just what to say to eventually get me to say yes. One day, he approached me and asked, "What do you think about us getting into boating?"

Well, I thought to myself, *I don't think I like the water.*

I wasn't crazy about the idea. I really had nothing to reflect back on in this field. My family didn't have the funds or an interest in water activities, so it was foreign to me. The closest I ever got to water was an above-ground pool, and I enjoyed that.

So, of course, we bought a twenty-eight-foot boat.

Over time, we upgraded to a forty-six-foot boat, and I have to admit, I enjoyed our ability to escape the ordinary to enjoy our special life. The girls enjoyed it and learned a lot. That was the best way to describe Don, always moving and learning something new. Nothing scared him or held him down. Snowmobiles also became part of our world, and again, when he asked me about getting into that sport, I thought in my head, *It's cold out there, ugh.* We ended up doing that for years.

A perfect example of my husband's calming and non-excitable personality brings me to a great memory. Every few years, Don would move us up a size. Each time we moved up, the boat was more comfortable, and by the third boat, we had a thirty-four-foot Cruiser. We were able to fit the entire family on it for cruising and anchoring in the waters of Lake Ontario.

One summer day, we had about twenty family members on the boat in Sodus Bay. What a wonderful time; everyone was sun-kissed, and we had just finished eating at a restaurant located in the bay, and now we were on our way back to our dock. A perfect day, ending in a perfect way, until Don asked me if I could take the wheel.

"Something is in my eye. I need to remove my contact," he told me and then instructed me to stay close to the buoy.

Pretty easy instruction, I thought. However, despite my confidence, I still hit the ground, which in turn jerked the boat back and then forward and killed the engines.

As Don ran upstairs—after hitting his face on the mirror when we jerked forward and back—he asked what happened.

I told him, "Shit, we hit ground, and I am as close to the buoy as possible!"

In a calm tone, he just said, "It's the wrong side of the buoy."

I then responded, "You didn't tell me which side."

He turned around to check on the family, and he said it looked as if they were posing for a family photo, just staring and waiting for him to explode. This was just not in his nature—to explode or yell or scream. He always composed himself, and this was his way, both in front of people and behind closed doors. He obviously wasn't thrilled by the accident, but his mindset was first things first, the safety of everyone, and he would deal with the needed repairs afterward.

Don maneuvered the boat off the ground and got one engine started, and we slowly made our way back to the dock. As the family was leaving, my sister-in-law looked at me and said, "He didn't even yell at you." I simply nodded. This was Don's way of dealing with the problem and moving on. Why escalate the current situation and add to the misery of the problem? What's done is done, so move on. Don's calm nature made our family outings enjoyable and always entertaining. The adventures we embarked on were irreplaceable. The bond we built will hopefully last forever.

We brought our girls with us everywhere, and they were part of every experience we had. We were a family, and that's what families do. Never say no. Try it; you might like it. Experiences build your journey, and we did everything in our power to include the girls and open their eyes to every possible horizon.

During the summers, we boated. We traveled across the lake, taking on adventures and showing them new places, which included multiple trips to Canada.

In the winter, we would travel to Old Forge, where the roads were used as snowmobile trails. The snowfall was at least double the snowfall we experienced in Rochester, and as you gazed across any area in Old Forge, it was like entering a white heaven, never-ending and glistening.

In the months during school, the girls were involved in not only school sports but also danced for a couple of different dance studios. It was never-ending. The activities they were involved in kept us constantly moving and left little downtime. Don and I both agreed that being busy was good. Activities are good, and family time is the most important—that was really the most important lesson we wanted to impress upon our children.

When you reflect back on your spouse or partner, there are events or conversations that took place that bring a smile to your face. These memories tend to shed light on who that person really was with you behind closed doors. Don was a true romantic. He enjoyed the movies that always ended as the Hallmark channel designed, happy and together. He also enjoyed watching a few of my favorite TV shows, one being *Sex in the City*. Of course, he had his snide comments, but he enjoyed the twisted scenes that ended with couples coming together.

He would bring me roses just because. He would surprise me with a call or text message just to say he missed me. Unannounced, he would show up at my office to take me to lunch.

Don practiced so many little touches throughout our lives. He would ask the silliest questions, like, "Why do you love me?"

I would respond seriously, saying, "I don't know why. I just love you to the moon and back, and we were meant to be together." He, of course, could list all the reasons why he loved me. Who does that!? I used to call him "The Machine," meaning methodical and always consistent. An over-thinker, yes, I would describe him as one of those, too.

Our favorite times were the simple ones. Every Friday night when the TV show *Dallas* aired, we were sure to be home with the kids fed and in bed, and then Don would cook up a gourmet meal. Don could cook and was a wizard at blending flavors. He learned from his mom, who was a great cook. We would sit on the floor, eat our meals, and watch our favorite show. This was such a highlight for us. We never minded being alone together; we actually preferred it. We were our own best time.

Don was calming. I could breathe easier when I was in his presence. He relaxed me. I am always running at hyper-speed, and he was the complete opposite. He walked slower, and he talked slower. I often thought to myself, *How in the hell does he complete what he sets out to do in a timely manner?* But he always did. I could never figure that out. He was a natural teacher, an educator of both life and business. He used the platforms of many different businesses to hone his skills.

He was a giver and caretaker, which was evident when his parents fell ill, and he alone took on the responsibility of their care. He was kind-hearted and wanted others to succeed. At work, he could be tough and demanding at times, but the business world was a different kind of animal that needed to be dealt with in a different manner. He was opinionated and thought he knew everything. He was a kid at heart with a wild spirit. He didn't project this image very often to others, but life with Don was fun.

They say the way someone doodles during conversations says a lot about that person. He always doodled, and I realized after attending his weekly Wednesday sales meetings that his paperwork was full of arrows pointing in all directions. Sometimes, words were attached or located by certain patterns, but for the most part, there were just arrows and movement, lots of movement. I sat back one day and thought that drawing was like our life: unpredictable but predictable, all over the place but with definite direction and goals.

Our life together was full of new adventures, like the time we woke up one Sunday morning and decided to go to the health club that we belonged to, with plans to get a workout in, only to find the doors locked and a sign on the building stating, "Out of Business." Don investigated this, only to find out that the situation was between the health club owner and the building owner. After many meetings with both men, Don came to me and said, "I think it's time we open our own health club."

I thought to myself, *Now, that's a great idea.* Then asked, "Where are we going to get the money for that?"

He responded with the same confidence he always had, telling me, "If we have pre-sign-ups and commitments from members, we will be fine." I trusted his business judgment and felt fortunate to be part of this adventure. Everything was a stepping stone for Don, not a stumbling block. We would just keep building, and we were fortunate to enjoy the journey and never let the journey defeat us. WE HAD IT ALL.

In 1995, we opened up a health club named Metro Fitness. The facility offered thirty-six aerobic and step classes, free weights, and cardio machines and could house about five hundred members. Located in Country Village, we had access to most of the lower level of this location so we could offer many amenities to our members. We owned and operated it for ten years. This was such a passion of ours, and we both enjoyed it.

The corporation's name was selected by Don, PAS Corp, for Patricia Ann Salamone. I was shocked and touched by this. Owning a health club required some certificates acknowledging that your staff was qualified to teach. I remember when Don and I were studying for the Athletics and Fitness Association certification, which was required to teach classes. One evening, as I was attempting to study, he looked at me and asked me if I needed help, and he said he had a process that worked every time. My response was, as always, with a little bit of an attitude. "I can handle it. I think I know how to study."

In the end, I passed and Don did not. The college graduate needed to repeat the test.

I enjoyed that victory, and trust me, I continually rubbed it in his face for a long time. He did eventually pass, but I could never graciously let that pass by.

This outlet reinforced our desire to stay healthy and have fun doing it. I ran the day-to-day functions, and Don handled the business portion. The negotiations that took place on the rent, the unruly customers, you name it, we dealt with it. We did this together, and I learned a lot from Don during this time.

He was surprisingly willing to turn over responsibilities to me before I was willing to take them on. There are certain special memories that stir an inner smile in me even today when I think of them. These are the memories that I will hold dear forever.

If you have ever taught an aerobics class, it's about timing and building a move off of the previous move. This is how Don worked.

Owning a health club—next move.

Mixing his own music—next move.

Selling his mixed tapes to other instructors in the city—everything was a branch of opportunity for Don to tap into.

As we continued on our life's journey, there came a time when our business was stressed. At this time, Don also owned and operated a home improvement distribution business, DC Distributing, which acted as a middleman. Don bought and housed materials and then sold them to contractors doing home improvement on residential homes, which included windows and siding. The market was tough, and consumer buying and confidence were down. It was a good time for Don to rethink his position in the market. Additionally, he had taken on a partner, and that ended ugly. That's what happens when the reality of your partner stealing from you becomes evident. Thankfully, an opportunity came knocking on our door. Don was offered the opportunity to join an organization in the home improvement industry, which he was knowledgeable in. The organization seemed pretty solid, so he took the offer, but not as an owner, which was new for Don. He wasn't thrilled with this, but he went along. He learned the retail business and assisted in growing that business to double-digit growth. This was the beginning of our new future. Wholesale to retail, now that's a leap of faith.

Don never gave himself room for failure. It was always onward and upward, even if it meant taking a few steps back to gain entry into a different type of business where all the margins were different. In wholesale, he acted as a distributor, but retail involves direct sales to consumers. This was a different business model and required a different sales strategy. That's the beauty of possessing a patient mindset. Slow and steady wins the race; sprinters are just that, sprinters, and they putter out quickly. This was an opportunity to meet others who were already successful and get his name in the field that he eventually soared in. There were bumps and bruises, but we survived and forged forward.

Don may have had some anxiety over this change, but he never showed it. He was not one to dwell on the difficulties of change. He just forged ahead, knowing the time served would eventually give him the results he was ultimately striving for.

Nightmares come in many forms, and I'm having the worst imaginable.

Forty-one years together, what just happened? Please, wake me up!

Reality is nowhere in sight. I can't grasp the facts because they can't be true. I'm feeling beyond grief-stricken. I am at a total loss of who I am and where I am going.

The events of January 17th cannot be real. Please, help me. I think I'm going crazy.

I am numb; I feel nothing. I'm going through the movements, which mean nothing to me now. I'm forever wanting to go back to sleep and have this be over. My fears are slowly attacking me, like a terrorist that has gained control over all that I know.

What is going on? What do I do?

Flurries of thoughts I can't control . . .

"The greatest lesson I have learned in life is that I still have a lot to learn."

—Steven Covey

Chapter 5

THE RETAIL MONSTER

DON'S DAYS WERE spent becoming familiar with retail sales, which is quite different from wholesale. In the home improvement industry, be it siding or windows, completion is ultimately the most important thing. Don always made sure he understood the consumer's wants and needs so he could meet their expectations. This involved being aware of their financial situations and how they were going to afford the improvement. If the consumer voiced that they needed or wanted assistance in this area, Don would introduce alternative financial packages to consumers. He had to have a thorough understanding of the packages to help guide them through this part of the process. Affordability is part of the sale. If customers know they can afford the improvement, they have little else to think about. Meanwhile, he was making another move.

After taking the time to understand retail and observe its ebbs and flows, Don decided that this business model was the one he wanted to invest his time and energies in. The marketplace was in desperate need of good contractors who took care of their customers. Building a good reputation with a solid product enabled growth in many areas. Once he became more experienced in the industry, he took another position at a new company. He joined up with two heavy hitters in the home improvement industry located in Massachusetts and extending all the way to Albany. Don's growth was plotted to penetrate the Western New York area, including Binghamton and Syracuse.

During this time, Don worked closely with one of the owners, who took him under his wing. Their chemistry was remarkable, something I had not seen before. It took a lot for Don to be inspired by someone, and this relationship possessed all the right ingredients. This self-made millionaire had the patience and the ability to teach, and Don was a willing and able student. He absorbed all the information and put into practice all that was shown to him. Don completely trusted his mentor and took his word as gospel. During this time, Don's knowledge and confidence grew every day.

The company was doing extremely well, but there was tension between the two owners. A business can only function so long as the culture remains positive. Another great characteristic of Don was his ability to read the tea leaves. He was monitoring the self-destruction of this company closely and had already made a decision to follow his mentor if they split. So, when the split eventually did happen, Don had already made his intentions evident to the one he intended to follow. The next few months were ugly, and Don, at that point, was intertwined in so many areas of the business. He knew he had to decisively and delicately remove himself in the time frame that worked financially for us.

Numbers never lie, and don't fool with the system. These are the words that Don lived by. Don followed the direction of his mentor and joined a new organization, New England Sash, which was young, enthusiastic, and growing. The owner was about the same age as me, and he was a special kind of person. Although extremely business-minded and hard-headed, he was a kind soul, and I liked him very much.

Don had become a hot commodity with his knowledge of building and maintaining a strong, confident sales staff. He was a great salesman and educator, and he knew how to get his point across to many different types of learners. Let's face it: by this time, he'd had years to practice on me.

Don once told me that when he was in college, a professor pulled him aside, and I quote, said, "Don't worry, Donald, it's the C students that rule the world." I believe, at this time in his life, he was just starting to understand that it had not been an insult as he had thought. Success is truly about the determination and inner strength to never give up. Juggling was just part of our life.

At the same time, our girls were getting older, and the housewife thing was not fulfilling my desire to challenge myself. I was getting bored, and Don knew it before I did. I loved being home raising my girls, but with them in school full-time, I needed more. I was ready for a new chapter in my life.

Fortunately, Don had an idea—an opportunity in the mortgage industry. When it was difficult for certain consumers to get approved through the normal channels of financing for home improvements, they would work with a mortgage broker. Don was currently working with an individual who worked for a mortgage broker, and he often would come home and say, "I think this is something you would enjoy, and I know you would be great at it."

He even went so far as to mention to one of the owners of the mortgage company, The Ambassador Group, that his wife would be such an asset to their organization. The next thing I knew, there was to be an informal interview. I was to be interviewed by the two female owners at Big Boy's Restaurant, which was set up by Don. I was so nervous. I really didn't have any knowledge of mortgages other than the bills you pay monthly to keep your house. I couldn't even remember the last time I'd thought about creating a resume, and what would I put on it? Great mommy for the last twelve years?

Despite my nerves, it went well. I was so relaxed by the time the interview ended, and to my relief, they offered me a position at their company as a mortgage originator. It was a new beginning for me. Hired and trained, I was working with the best mortgage originators out there. This was one of the largest mortgage brokers in the city, and they had influence. The owners were wonderful and caring, and the staff was energetic and hungry. This opportunity gave me confidence and knowledge I would have never gained elsewhere. I loved this job and made many friendships that have lasted the test of time.

Flourishing at this position, I was one of the top five originators out of about sixteen. Meeting a lot of different people and being able to help a lot of consumers with their financial situations was so gratifying. This was during the subprime days, and there was plenty to go around. Many homeowners were looking to re-finance or re-mortgage their current homes to take advantage of cash-out or complete home improvements. This was not a job, but a career that I loved. I felt that I had blossomed.

I was very fortunate to have a husband who thought the world of me and believed in me more than I believed in myself. He saw my talents way before I did. He was my mentor and my biggest fan, and he was the sole reason I was able to join the workforce with confidence and succeed as I did. Early on, Don came to the conclusion that he was going to involve me in every aspect of his life. He brought me with him on leads, and I was involved in all the decisions. I didn't realize my ability to absorb information until I found myself reflecting back on past situations with Don and using that knowledge in the future.

Our lives were flourishing on every level. Our family life was good, affected only by normal struggles, and work was going well and keeping us busy. Over the last five years, Don reached every goal set out in front of him, growing with knowledge and confidence. As I have mentioned before, his mind never stopped. He was consistently attempting to plant a seed in my head that we would make great work partners. He continued to remind me that an opportunity was available for me to join forces with the company he worked for. His slight pressure eventually led me to accept an interview at the company he worked for. After the interview, I reluctantly accepted a position to handle the consumer financing division. The timing was ideal, actually. Subprime lending was drowning. The year 2008 was tough for many, and it was becoming more difficult to do mortgages that included cash-out for home improvements. The banks were tightening up, and the timing was perfect to move on. This is when I learned about alternative financing and programs for consumers. I was now intertwined with Don, striving for the same goals. This was an extremely difficult decision for me as I had made so many friends and I really loved what I was doing, but I knew in my heart of hearts this was the perfect time to make the switch to a new company, and I felt I was up for the challenge.

Working together was not a new thing for us. It takes incredible control and attention to detail to divide responsibilities so that all the business's needs are being met. Don was actually better at this, but I slowly learned to be more efficient and let go of the need to micromanage everything. Living with the person you work with takes patience, understanding, and the ability to turn off the work part of your life and transition to the personal part. This was something we learned when we first started our health club, and we strengthened these skills as we started this new endeavor together.

Working for a retail sales organization was ideal for Don. He was a born salesperson. He would say, "It's about the quality of the product and your personal character. Put the needs of the consumer first, always first." He was as genuine as they came, and consumers knew this after meeting with him. "Rid yourself of the car salesman illusion," he would tell his sales staff.

When I was fortunate enough to be able to go on leads with him, I got the perfect opportunity to witness how he actually worked his "magic." He enjoyed meeting with potential clients, planning their spending, and giving them the most value for their dollar. It enhanced the value of their biggest asset, their home. The product was always one of the best on the market.

He made the consumer feel confident that the purchase made sense for their world, financially and aesthetically. Of course, functionality also came into the picture.

Direct sales is not an easy way to earn a living. It took immense focus and dedicated hours of training and evolving. When I was with him on his leads, whether we had a sale or not, it was always a pleasant visit, and all parties were very respectful of each other. At that time, being involved in so many aspects of Don's days didn't seem so important, but today, those experiences are vital for survival.

This life is a gift, and the successes are measured. Money, titles, and power are the measures so many people use to gauge their success in life. These in and of themselves are not bad, but they should not be the core of your life. To evolve to higher levels, you must realize that the importance of those things is minor compared to the growth of your heart, your knowledge, and your thirst to learn more. Forgiving, accepting, and not judging others is the standard that we must strive for. As Robert Brault said, "Appreciate the little things, for one day you may look back and find they were the big things."

We are all one and connected, all with individual struggles. What truly makes you special is the acceptance that all of this is about *love*.

Grief becomes your companion.

My thoughts are not my friends. My personal travels down this black hole abruptly bring me back to the realization that I am alone. I am without my soulmate, my partner for life. Put aside all your great memories; it's easy to be swept away into the swirling downward vacuum of your thoughts. After losing someone that was your everything, you eventually realize or hope that there has to be a bigger something, somewhere. There has to be a new beginning of incomprehensible beauty, love, and connection.

Beauty, in all ways, that we can barely touch, see, or feel here on this planet. Blind faith needs to be accessed now. This ultimately tests all your beliefs. You question your core beliefs, and you open up to the unknown.

This can't be the end.

I feel this belief is our playground of rides that take us in many directions, and how we land is up to us.

I can't even express the emptiness, anger, and confusion, flooded by bitterness, that runs through every inch of my being. I am destroying all that I was, and I know I can't live like that. I'm determined to become me again.

Strike a new balance! How the hell do you do that? These are such unfamiliar feelings. Fear now plays a big role in my life; this, too, is an unfamiliar feeling. My new mantra is "Conceal, don't feel." Sometimes, your toughest times are your memories.

I feel mentally exhausted and constantly jittery, two different feelings completely taking control of me—calm me down, please.

"You won't always be motivated;
you must learn to be disciplined."

—Denzel Washington

Chapter 6

THE "C" WORD

LIFE WAS CLICKING along. Our girls were wonderful on every level. Watching them grow up was exhilarating and, frankly, a lot of fun, They both possessed a sense of humor, and they shared their most important moments in their life with us. I think all parents think that, and I guess what we don't know doesn't hurt us. Kids will be kids, and I'm sure my girls pushed the envelope on a few things, but we always had an understanding that the truth over anything else was the most important thing and that we were always there for them.

Dating was another fun aspect of bringing up two girls. Why is it that their choices never really line up with what the parent expects? There were plenty of "interesting" situations, but Don and I got through them, as all parents do. I could see the wheels turning in Don's head as soon as we would meet a "new one," and I knew it was going to be a long night. Don and I definitely had different approaches to raising our daughters, and I have to say, he was more successful than me at getting them to make the right decision. There was one situation when I thought I had really done all that I could to help my daughter realize what a loser she was dating. I even purchased a book titled *Red Flags That You're Dating a Loser*, and then I highlighted everything I thought pertained to this individual. Well, that didn't go over so well, and Don had to step in and clear the way, and eventually, he got her head in the right place.

Both girls were involved in sports, primarily soccer, and it was important to us that a parent was at their games, even if it meant splitting up to catch their games. I was the loud one, and Don was the pacer. He never yelled, and I was never sure how he composed himself so well. I had to work on that, I guess, but I was not a fan of overzealous players who were extremely physical on the field, especially when it came to contact with my girls.

Due to their embarrassment, after their games, they would mention that they could hear my voice clearly on the field, and although they appreciated my enthusiasm, they often asked if I would take it down a level or two.

I would just respond, "Very funny," and then attempt to explain my reaction, telling them that the other player was brutal and rough. They just rolled their eyes at me.

Meanwhile, work was demanding, but its growth was amazing. Don had reached the proposed goals for the New York Division, so the sky was the limit. Then, as life often does, it threw us a gut punch.

One day, my mom asked out of the blue if I had scheduled a mammogram. I thought to myself, *Why would she ask that question?* I was only forty-one years old, and I had done a baseline the previous year. I responded, "No, I haven't."

Her immediate response was, "Well, do it."

I always felt my mom was psychic or extremely intuitive when it came to her kids, so I booked my appointment. The day of the appointment was as ordinary as they came, with the exception of the doctor calling my name to come back to her office just as my hand was reaching for the office door to leave. Boom, the thought hit me: she saw something suspicious on the film. Indeed, she wanted more tests.

This led to more appointments and a diagnosis of breast cancer.

Don had a direct conversation with the surgeon and asked him the question, "If this was your wife, what would you do?"

His answer was not what I expected at all. He said there was a ninety-nine percent survival rate with complete removal of the breast. I plummeted. Don's reaction was that there was nothing more important than my life.

Whatever it takes. It's just a body part that held little importance compared to our life together.

Scary doesn't even describe what it felt like to hear this kind of information. It took me a long time to emotionally adjust to this reality, but through it all, my husband never wavered. He was my rock. After multiple conversations about our ability to carry on our lives together, Don had me accepting and realizing how fortunate we were that this had a ninety-nine percent survival rate. It was important for us to accept whatever needed to be done and move on. We had so much to look forward to and so much living to do.

He got me through this terrible time and made me realize this was just going to be a small blip in our journey. We had a great family and a great life, and we needed to move on and hopefully never look back. As stupid as this may seem, I threw out the clothes I wore to the initial screening, thinking that would protect me from ever going through that horrible moment again. I survived my cancer scare with the love and strength of family, and, as always, in the blink of an eye, time passed by so quickly.

Today, I sit back, and I realize I did not entertain the idea that I had the "paradox of choice" when Don passed.

This is probably the best thing that could have happened to me.

I had to continue on with my life for so many reasons.

I forced myself to live out a life that mattered. There has to be a reason for this. What is the purpose of this? What do I need to experience and learn? What in the hell did I sign up for in this next chapter of my life?

If I could redo my contract with God, I would change this ending.

What is my life's plan? I know after educating myself that this time here is to grow, learn, and help others with an open heart and an understanding that we are all in this together.

"Don't use energy to worry, use your energy to believe, create, trust, grow and HEAL."

—Franklin Roosevelt

Chapter 7

GROWING OUR FAMILY

THE GENTLEMAN WHO owned New England Sash (N.E.S.), the company Don and I worked for, was one year younger than me. He was, for the most part, a kind-hearted and good businessman. I got along with him, and he was always kind to me. He was tracking twenty-two million dollars in sales for three products. At this point, Don was running a sales staff of over forty people and traveling between New York and Massachusetts.

The company spanned over five states, and the growth was unprecedented. Everyone involved felt the benefits of this, including Don and I. This was an awakening for us on many levels. Lots of money, lots of politics, and lots of learning. Don was always prepared to maneuver around the politics to prevent as much damage to the company and its people as possible. His job was to ensure that sales came in and they were profitable. Remember, numbers never lie, and decisions should be based solely on the numbers. You can determine so much by sorting through the reports and the numbers.

Don't fool with the system; it's time-tested. Or, as I saw it, don't fool with the Salamones. Don was on a mission, and he was committed to completing the task at hand and achieving all of his goals. He devoted all of his time and energy to this.

Meanwhile, on a personal level, our daughter Nicole was getting married. The wedding date of August 27, 2005, was approaching quickly. The details and planning went as smoothly as can be expected. The groom was involved in every step, which was greatly appreciated. They both had definite ideas and concerns, and it was amazing to watch them navigate the discussions and decisions that needed to be made. At the time, I wished I could slow down the process. I wasn't mentally ready to accept the fact our daughter was getting married. Where had the time gone?

All the planning reminded me of their first date, which, unfortunately for our daughter, had been chaperoned by her parents. Hilariously, we arrived at the same restaurant at the same time.

When we walked in and spotted them waiting at the end of the bar, Don made his way to them and asked, "Why don't we sit together?"

The response, although a bit delayed, was, "Sure."

Don was aware of Kevin's hand on Nicole's knee, which was not something he appreciated, and of course, he pointed that out to me. Once seated, my daughter excused herself to run to the bathroom, and there we sat with this complete stranger, struggling to find things to talk about. Awkward is putting it mildly, not for us, but for this young man. Kevin was polite and didn't get flustered. He took the conversation in stride, and we enjoyed his company. By the end of the evening, Don and I both felt comfortable with the prospect of their relationship getting serious.

A son-in-law, how exciting! Don loved the idea of finally having a guy to hang out with. Don was all about his girls; he lived for them, and he would have done anything for them.

He never wavered in his beliefs, likes, or dislikes. At times, he was stubborn and old-fashioned. Sometimes, his thought processes were a little outdated to me, and I attribute that to our age difference. He did, however, have an amazing and remarkable patience. He would talk a situation to death; he peeled every layer of the onion. My daughters related to him on a different level, and our parenting system seemed to have worked.

My only hope now is that I am enough for them. To be there for them and help them through all their difficult times. The loss of their dad has been devastating. I believe both of my daughters are very capable of working through difficult situations, but something like this, so unexpected and sudden, would devastate anyone and rock their world. I believe they are both resilient and strong, but my concern is that they are consumed with worry about me. We are all trying to deal with our grief while simultaneously trying not to add our grief burden to each other.

My days now are occupied by work. The business is exploding. My nights are long and difficult. My mind doesn't know how to shut down. Once I do achieve sleep, that is when Don visits me. Many dreams are filled with messages, direct messages. So clear and precise, there is no way to deny them. His guidance and an outpouring of love are what I wake up to now.

Believe what you will, but there is life after death. I am a firm believer. Please accept the information out there and educate yourself. I have had dreams from Don that have come true, and I have received wisdom that goes beyond what I am capable of on my own. I have been comforted at the most needed times.

"You only have three choices in life, give up, give in, or give it all you have."

—Charleston Parker

Chapter 8

BEACH HOUSE

DON DESERVES THE credit for our upward movement. I was overly comfortable where we were in all stages of our lives, but Don just kept going, and he now had this crazy idea to live on the water. Uprooting and moving houses at this time in our lives was not on my radar, and in an attempt to slow him down, I came up with a list of requirements that I would want if he wanted me to even consider moving.

The most important parameter for him to follow was, of course, location. I recommended a stretch of Beach Avenue between the beach side and Ling Road, about twenty miles from our current house. Of course, he made it his daily ritual to drive through that area, and it ended up being fruitful for him.

One morning, just as he drove by, a real-estate agent was pounding a for sale sign into the ground, smack in the middle of my preferred location! Don got out of his car, spoke with the agent, and had me back there within a few hours. From the road, I could see it was a large home that would require a ton of renovation. We got out of our truck, and then Don put his hands over my eyes. He guided me to the back of the property, uncovered my eyes, and said, "Now, let me ask you, can you imagine looking at this every day?"

Once I slowly opened my eyes, I was taken aback by the peaceful, restful waters that lay in front of me. The beautiful scene immediately relaxed me, and I looked at Don and said, "It's perfect." I knew at that time how much this move would mean to Don. To go to these extremes to get my approval said it all. I needed no other convincing that this direction was the right one for us.

That was it. The deal was done, and the property was ours. Don had that house torn down, and we built a home designed by both of us. We chose a three-story design so that we could have as much square footage as possible. The lots on Beach Avenue are on the narrow side, so we decided to build up. We also decided to have a walk-out lower level. I am not a fan of the word "basement," and if you want to utilize as much square footage as we had planned, the lower level had to be as well designed as the rest of the house. We were the only ones on Beach Avenue to have full access to the beach. A very unique property.

Imagine, if you would, waking up to a landscape that made you feel like you were on vacation every day. It took nine months to complete, and we were in heaven. I never saw Don so delighted and proud of a home. This property turned out to be exceedingly functional for us, and we had many family gatherings and parties there.

Meanwhile, work was getting tense. There was something in the air. Don was uncomfortable with the conversations that took place when he met with the owners of the company that we worked for. His sixth sense was telling him this had a shelf life.

The owner was looking to get out of the business and retire. *What the hell?* He was only forty-eight years old! He claimed he was having heart palpitations. I'm not sure if that was the truth or not, but it was his decision. We all had to live with it. After months of negotiating, he finally gave us the New York division to carry on. Here we go again. Being an entrepreneur seemed to be Don's destiny.

The first year was a struggle: new house, new business, and now, we both had to work at building a company that had to support the lifestyle we were used to. When you own your own business, there is no time clock; it's what you put into it, so don't waste your time watching the clock. We were fortunate enough not to have to take money out of the business the first year. Our mindset was to build and grow. Don concentrated on sales and structure, and I assisted in finance, marketing, and administration. As history would have it, we slowly pulled ourselves out and just did what was necessary. Don always said, "Slow and steady wins the race." Well, this period of time was a testament to that.

Some days are better than others. I often feel that I am fumbling through them. People have told me I am so strong. If they only knew. I don't feel strong.

Most of the time, I don't feel anything. The world keeps turning, with people doing whatever they normally do, and I feel like I am stuck at the top of a Ferris wheel, with just the swaying cart.

I hate Ferris wheels.

"Having a powerful enough WHY will provide
you with the necessary HOW."

—Tony Robbins

Chapter 9

DISCOVERY DAY

OUR COMPANY'S RATE of growth was consistent year over year. We were financially solid and had taken a not-so-good reputation to one that was recognized as one of the best by those in the market. The only way to achieve this is by standing by your work and supporting the consumer. The consumer's experience has to be the foundation of your culture. Previously, this industry had a difficult time maintaining consumer confidence. Many consumers had been abused in some way, either because of poor quality work or the delayed completion of their projects. So, earning an A-rating with the Better Business Bureau and treating our customers right allowed for opportunities. As our business grew, we earned more market share and good consumer ratings, which led to industry recognition.

That is when Don was approached by an individual from an organization called Renewal by Andersen (RBA), a full-service window replacement division for the Andersen Corporation. The Andersen Corporation is an international window and door manufacturing enterprise whose headquarters are in Bayport, Minnesota. This individual expressed that he felt Don would be a perfect fit for their organization. He believed Don's leadership skills and business philosophies coupled well with the RBA world. Don was already familiar with the name Renewal by Andersen, and without delay, he reached out to RBA's corporate network for a meeting. Once an appointment was scheduled, we were given an agenda to tour the manufacturing plant and then commence the meeting to discuss all parties' intentions. Discovery Day was the title given to this agenda.

If Don was nervous, he didn't show it. He just presented our business model to them with confidence and reassured them that we could benefit from this venture, and so could they. We understood and acknowledged that this was an amazing opportunity, and we would not disappoint. It was evident that our intention was to grow the Western New York area, which was one of RBA's objectives. They were all about market share and continued consumer confidence in the name of Andersen.

After consideration, we were welcomed to the Renewal family in the RBA Division of the Rochester area. Although this was an amazing opportunity, the territory was not sufficient for Don. He wanted more, and within one year, we had all of Western New York. Business growth is a funny thing. It happens right in front of your eyes, and all of a sudden, it takes off, and you better hold on! We were experiencing growth in every department and had to move the business to a bigger facility with an eye for even more growth in the future. Two cities, two buildings, and lots of employees. Don and I were split between departments, taking on all the responsibility. Over time, we managed to hire outstanding people who assisted in our growth and helped us achieve the next level.

This was the strongest organization I had ever come across. Corporate's leadership and direction were outstanding. The people at the corporate level always shared best practices and did all they could to educate and support all affiliates and their continued growth.

We brought our younger daughter, Christine, on board, and she flourished and grew every day. Just watching her blossom was enough for me. She connected well with her dad on a business level, and he wanted to teach her as much as he could, starting her at the ground level and working her way up. When Christine was first brought in, she started as a marketing assistant and scheduled events for the company. In the marketing department, she had to deal with employee scheduling for events, negotiations with the vendors, and the logistics of set-up and take-down. The optimal goal was to walk away with a list of potential customers that we could contact at a later date. As she grew, she eventually moved into the position of manager for the service department, where it was all about communication, patience, and product knowledge. This experience launched her career and eventually led her to run the production department. Christine is very much like her father. Like her sister, Nicole, both girls are quick learners and have a talent for dissecting a department and bringing it to a higher level of performance. Christine had to experience life at RBA on every level, and that she did.

When it came to running a business together, Don and I blended well. As I stated before, I truly enjoyed working with my husband. His humor kept the day from getting too heavy to deal with. His calm attitude helped me learn that there actually is a better management style other than screaming. We complimented each other in a lot of ways and had the same core goals. It never consumed us at home. We just rolled with the daily challenges as if they were stepping stones to maneuver over. Once in a while at our workplace, he would turn to me and say, "You can't talk to me like we are sitting at our kitchen table!" Honestly, I found that comical, but I also knew he was right!

RBA's continuous growth over the years was double-digit. Business success is all about people, people, people, and more people. You need to find the right person for the right position, which is not an easy task and consists of reviewing numerous resumes. There are so many job seekers who look perfect on paper but don't really want to engage in their employment.

"Live and learn" was my motto when it came to hiring. I admit I made a few mistakes, but as the company continued to grow, we were fortunate to be able to work through the bad and find the diamonds in the rough.

Training and continuous hiring in every department had been the agenda for 2018, and in 2019, it was even more important. Preparing the new budget for 2019 was underway. The year was ending, and we didn't quite hit Don's goal of twenty million; we were a touch short. Although we'd experienced double-digit growth, Don was visibly upset about the shortfall. He had so much confidence in the selected teams, and he felt they were capable of so much more.

He looked at me one day in the office and said, "I feel as though there isn't a problem or situation that I can't get us through."

He had taken on all the problem situations and taught each manager how to resolve them and move forward. Our company attitude was clear: no situation was bigger than our willingness to fix it. The teams we put together had the commitment to work toward a common goal, focusing on satisfaction for all involved, including the customer and the company. Don was a master at placing the responsibility on the managers to resolve the daily issues. This meant they might not reach a satisfactory end result on the first attempt, but it exposed where the manager needed to grow and made them realize that continued effort and knowledge were necessary. The managers had to make an attempt, and if they failed, Don would obviously step in and help them adjust, but more importantly, they could use the example as a learning tool.

When we weren't working, we were taking on projects in our personal lives—like we didn't have enough to do. There was always constant motion, decisions, and changes taking place. Don never tired; he just kept the momentum moving forward in both our personal and professional lives.

Despite our business success, my instinct was nagging at me to convince Don to sell our property on Beach Ave, build a ranch in the Rochester area, and utilize our Florida vacation home that we had purchased a few years earlier as a getaway until retirement. This would reduce our tax burden by half, depending on the size of the ranch we built. He fought me tooth and nail for several different reasons. First off, the land we were looking at in Rochester was across the street from my eldest daughter and three grandkids. He thought being so close might cause an issue, and he was in love with the house on Beach Ave. He always said he was going to die in the beach house. It was his favorite home we ever built, with the best view of Lake Ontario. After continuous nagging, he finally agreed to move forward with my idea. I had this urge to be closer to our grand babies because a twelve-minute drive seemed so long!

I knew if I made the argument tie into a financial win, he would eventually come around. Remember, Don is all about the facts and numbers. He finally did come around, and he proceeded to purchase not only the lot for the build but an additional fourteen acres behind the house. This gave him the opportunity to place the house off the street. Not being directly across the street from the kids made him feel better. Building in a wooded lot would be a new adventure for us. Having access to fourteen additional acres offered a new kind of peace and relaxation filled with greenery and all that nature has to offer because God knows our love for land.

I began to see the wheels in Don's head start to ignite with ideas, and, of course, this included purchases of large equipment to assist in clearing off the land. Although we hired a builder, Don had to be part of it. He was like a big kid. Fortunately, he had the financial ability to aid his manly desires to purchase and operate large equipment. Eventually, he was able to use his equipment to clear the woods and make paths.

The plans for the new house were complete, and we did this side by side, designing our desires and watching them come to life on paper. Downsizing wasn't exactly the final outcome, but I also knew it wouldn't be. We were spoiled. We agreed not to put our current home on Beach Ave up for sale until the completion of the new build. My exact words to Don were, "I am definitely too busy and too old to have to worry about moving out to satisfy someone else's schedule." Financially, we could swing having both properties for a time, so we didn't burden ourselves with this added stress.

However, it was as if we never even had the conversation about waiting to sell the beach house because the next thing I knew, Don was introducing me to his hairdresser, who dabbled in real estate sales. It was as though I had never said anything, but of course, I went along. I had lived with a sales-oriented individual for many years, and I knew he would push his agenda nonstop, so I just saved the energy. His words did make sense. "What do we have to lose?"

The meeting was set, and as I glanced out of my dining room window, there came the entourage of interested buyers. When I opened the front door, I was completely taken aback. I knew the woman who expressed interest in my home. I had met her through one of my close friends, Sharon. This woman was Sharon's cousin, and we occasionally met her for drinks after work. She was extremely friendly, and I immediately felt a kinship to her and enjoyed her company. When I opened my door and she was standing there, her presence had a calming effect on me, and I'm not sure why. The conversation flowed with ease. We were two old friends who hadn't seen each other and had a lot of time to make up for. It only took one visit, and the house was sold. Don was considerate of my request not to rush us out, and we got them to agree not only on price but also on our terms. It was a creative type of deal. Don was comfortable with that, but I questioned his intent, and his direct response to me was, "I just wanted this taken off our plate." I wondered why we had to worry about getting things off our plates.

Blessings come in many different forms. Sometimes, they prepare you for the painful reality of what is to come. I am here to say you don't know what your subconscious or intuition knows, but listen to your intuition. Don't fight it; embrace it.

As the New Year introduced itself, we felt we were ready. Don and I had finally agreed that this was the year to start our slow attempt to exit toward retirement. This decision would be introduced with a target date, which, up to this point, had not been discussed. Everything was falling into place. Our new build was underway, and the business was strong and growing. There was a lot of juggling of our time and energies, but this was exactly how Don and I rolled. This was why retirement was a difficult conversation for us. Our dedication and work ethic were mirrored. Our love for each other and our profoundly entangled relationship made it all come together. We achieved all that we had from the ground up, with no inheritance of gifts, just plain old hard work and commitment. What was ours was ours, earned the best way—the memory-making way.

I don't believe that Don was ready to leave here. His family, his obligations, his world as we knew it. Our life together was preparing for a new chapter, one that we were excited about. It's absurd to think we actually have any control over this decision, though. The reality is we really don't know, and if we did, we would live differently.

I believe there are external energies or connections, not necessarily out in the open, but working behind the scenes in an attempt to protect us from the impact coming our direction. We have to become aware of these external signs. They occur, and we don't realize it until we give ourselves the opportunity to slow down and recognize that there were signs from the unknown that we didn't understand at the time. The Universe is massive; we have to accept that all is one, connecting us to everything and not restricting us to just our own personal desires. Trust your intuition. Open yourself up and let in what is demanding to come in. Oftentimes, our personal reluctance leads us to overrule living our truths.

They say that time heals all, but I'm not really sure about that. Time gives us a chance to adjust to our new surroundings and hopefully grasp the true meaning of this existence. To be blessed, thankful, and grateful was my mindset, and it continues to be. I cannot allow the sadness and grief to take hold and destroy this.

I found a greeting card with a line that reflects my life with Don: "Once in a while, right in the middle of an ordinary life, love gives us a fairytale."

"Faith means that you have peace even when you don't have all the answers."

—Joyce Meyer

Chapter 10

THE LAST NIGHT

JANUARY 16, 2019, was a Wednesday, and this day will be burned into my memory forever.

At 8:45 a.m., Nicole called and was very upset. She had shut her car door on her index finger, and she was not sure how much damage was done. She thought the whole tip of her finger was nipped off and was bleeding profusely, so she headed to the emergency room. I immediately finished getting dressed and rushed downstairs to leave. I reached the door, hand on the knob, and then I turned around and looked at Don, who was standing at the kitchen counter with his glasses on, writing out the deposit slips for the business. He was aware of the situation, as he had heard me on the phone. I turned around and looked at him, then I darted back to give him a kiss. He smiled at me and said, "Go!"

I thought about this later. Normally, when it came to the kids, I would just fly out of the house, but this was different. My action was out of character.

After Nicole's accident, the day was as ordinary as the days go. She was fine, and she didn't lose any part of her finger. Work was work, and Don had taken off for the afternoon. He was with his older brother, Vinny, clearing the lot our new house was being built on with his new piece of equipment, of course. He actually saw Nicole and her daughter Tessa outside and asked her to hold his Rolex watch so nothing happened to it.

It was freezing outside, and he was out there for at least five hours. When he finally came home, I had made most of our dinner, but the pork chops had to be done on the grill. He was the griller in the household.

Once they were done and after he showered to warm up, we ate dinner together. He looked exhausted, and I told him he looked so tired. He told me that he'd let his brother sit in the heated machine and that he'd stood outside for the entire time doing the manual labor. He had hit his leg on something. He was not quite sure what exactly had happened, but he did have a bruise.

When I got up to clear the dishes, I looked at him and told him, "I trust all the decisions that you make for us, total trust." I don't even know why I said that; it was not prompted at all. During dinner, we had not discussed anything concerning decision-making. He stood up and looked down at me with a piercing, faraway look and then pulled me in for a long, warm hug. I remember feeling that hug through to my soul, and the look in his eyes was so piercing it went right through me. I felt it through my ribs to my back. He proceeded to go into our home office and play his guitar. He did this periodically, and I often just worked around the house. That evening, I decided to go into the office and listen to him. I never did that. I commented on how good he sounded, and I loved the songs he was playing. I recorded him, and, of course, he just made a face at me.

He was mellow that night. When it was time to retire, we always went to bed together unless there was a football game on. We got ready for bed, and he turned to me and said, "I recorded a movie for us tonight." The name of the movie was *Money Never Sleeps*.

I said, "Okay, that's great." Within minutes of the movie starting, he was snoring.

I was watching the movie, and about three-quarters through, he woke up and said, "Let's turn off the movie."

I responded, "It's almost over. I want to finish watching it."

He kissed me, and his last words to me were, "In our next life, we are coming back as stock brokers."

I responded, "We will make a great team."

Then, we kissed goodnight for the last time.

I woke up, and if I were to guess, it was probably around 3 a.m. I usually woke up once a night around that time and could see the moonlight gleaming through our bedroom sliding glass door. I never covered it up. The view of the lake was beautiful. The moonlight shined through on my side of the bed. I turned on my side, and I spoke to what I thought was my husband. I said, "What are you doing?" and then I remember nothing. It was like I was knocked out, forced back to sleep. It was the oddest thing, as though I wasn't supposed to see or remember this.

What I saw was a figure in white over my husband's body, no face, just a figure. I wasn't scared or alarmed. I just spoke to it, and then I remember, as I stated, nothing.

When the alarm went off at 7:30 a.m., I reached over to the nightstand and froze. The thought raced through my head. I knew my husband was gone. There was no reason for me to even think anything like this. It was just this sense of loss, of aloneness in my head. I slowly turned around and realized it was true.

I can't even begin to explain what happens to a person when they realize the love of their life, who is lying in bed next to them, is gone.

I frantically called 911, and I don't remember what happened from that point on. A blur of people, a blur of emotions. What I do remember is my oldest brother, Tony, coming to me and asking me to go with him to see Don for the last time. He held me tight as we went upstairs.

I knelt down next to my husband, crying. I kissed him, and then I bolted back up and looked at Tony. I'm not sure how many times I repeated, "Oh my God, he has black on!" and all the memories of the night before flooded me.

The figure that I saw in pure white was not Don.

I sit alone at night and reflect on many conversations. I remember after Don's passing, my mom looked at me one morning and said, "He must have been a great student to have learned all he had to in such a short period of time."

Her next sentiment was that the timing was out of place and that she should have gone before he did.

My eighty-eight-year-old mom was an amazing woman who I loved with my whole heart. Even in her fragile state, she was comforting me. I was brought up believing in life after death due to her. She believed and introduced this world to me at a young age. I attended and was allowed to miss school for many functions on this subject.

I had been with Don for forty-one years. He was all I knew, so this reality hit me hard. I believe Don lived his truth. He was complete in so many ways. I'm not saying perfect, but nobody is. Marriage is accepting, growing, and learning from each other. The reality is that those left behind suffer the impact of such a devastating loss alone. At times, you think your mind is playing games. If I could shut down these thoughts that haunt me, would the pain ever go away? What universal lessons are there to be learned from such a loss?

Your time here is a gift, and your journey is your own.

Regardless of the distractions in life, and there are as many as you can create in your mind, you will always feel the broken chain, the broken life, because it mirrors the broken person. Know that we all will experience losses throughout our lives. The world is constantly changing, and we have to adapt to it and make the most of it. This is a ride: either we attempt to accept the changes and move on or not!

Appreciation of all that touches you is so important. Little things that most fluff off are really the true moments that build your life's story. You are writing your own story; design it well and make it count.

"Every next level of your life will demand
a different you."

—Leonardo DiCaprio

Chapter 11

INTO THE UNKNOWN

AT FIRST, MY efforts were focused on detaching from reality and existing inside my protective barrier. There were nagging thoughts that propelled me forward, prompting me to accomplish what I nick-named "triumphs." Although these were very personal and probably seem very minuscule to most, they were my fears to deal with, and I knew I had to conquer them at some point. I realized this on the day of my husband's funeral. As the Catholic mass ended, there was a designated order for the precession to walk out of the church, and I was directly after the priest. I had to descend alone. This was the longest walk I had ever had to make alone. Others were supported by spouses and family, but I was alone in this, and I swear, as I glanced up to look at the designated walkway, it grew longer with every step I took. From that day, the "new norm" was something I had to embrace with or without understanding the why; I just had to accept it. Other triumphs for me were traveling alone, boarding an airplane alone, and the list continues on.

"Into the Unknown" was the theme for the company's Christmas party at the end of 2019. The theme couldn't have been more appropriate for me as a person or us as a company. Imagine, will you, the thoughts of all the employees at this time. Their leader, whom they loved dearly, their mentor, their friend, gone.

No warning, no preparation. The haunting look in their eyes showed true fear. I was questioning so many things at this point. What do I do? Do I possess what it requires to continue in this business? There were so many questions during a time when my focus was, at best, sixty percent. My attention was constantly blurred by other thoughts. There was really no one to talk to about my concerns and anxieties. My confidence was at an all-time low, realizing I was to embark into the unknown, and as the saying goes, you don't know what you don't know. You're either going to be inspired or intimidated, and I knew this was completely up to me to decide. I had to silence the whispers in my head and move forward.

I felt as if my two girls were suffering and that I wasn't there for them as much as I should have been. It was such a difficult time for all of us. Often, I felt inadequate and at a loss for answers. I needed to reinvent myself on a totally different level if I was to continue. I needed to keep myself busy and not get caught up in worrying about the results. I concentrated on creating a world in which I could function. The road to recovery lies in having the strength to get up and start planning out what to do next. As Deborah Wiles said, "Life is full of surprises, but the biggest one of all is learning what it takes to handle them." When life surprises you, it is vital to plan ahead and find the strength and the resources to keep going.

I chose to show up for work every day, and this was a blessing. It kept me busy and focused on moving forward. I would not allow my fears to take over and control me. Taking on additional roles in the company was inevitable. How would I fill the void, immerse myself, and be involved in all aspects of the business, from marketing to sales and production? I did these things by requiring more management meetings, attending the current ongoing meetings, and creating a culture that rang true to my beliefs. It required my complete involvement in all resolutions to help the company move forward.

RBA concluded 2019 by not only breaking Don's goal of twenty million, but we surpassed it by a million. The dedication and unwillingness to do less was prevalent among all employees. Many took on tasks beyond their training and showed me that together, we could accomplish more.

During the latter part of 2019, I was contacted by another affiliate who was looking to buy the territory and take over our location. I didn't share this with many. To sell or resign a new five-year contract with RBA was a nagging, persistent thought in my head, wreaking havoc on me. I did accept a couple calls from an interested party to discuss the possibility of selling, and on the second call, I realized it was not the direction for me. I wanted to do this. I needed to do this. Once I cemented that idea in my mind, there was no turning back. This was exactly what I needed. This was my new life going forward.

It's been slightly over one year since my husband passed. The move has paid dividends to me. My three grandkids, Micayla, Trevor, and Tessa, can easily visit since we live across the street from each other. They bring me such joy, companionship, and happiness. I am surrounded by my family, the most important people in my life. Our strength grows every day, and our memories of Don—my husband, my girls' dad, and papa—live on, and will forever.

Has it gotten easier? In some ways, yes, and in others, no. I think I deal with the day-to-day with a better understanding of the end. This is not a dark thought; the end is coming for all of us. Acknowledging that something is going to take place after our death should bring a sense of peace to all of us. There is a ton of information out there; you can't possibly read all there is. The reporting on near-death experiences (NDE) is remarkable. Spiritually accepting that this is not the end is a result of faith. This acceptance and belief are extremely helpful during the hopelessness we feel after losing a loved one. Explaining away the proof, I feel, is done by many for self-serving reasons, which I could equate to fear. My belief is that proof lies within all who accept the information that is easily accessible.

Many believe that this life is the largest event of all time, but consider there is a bigger and more beautiful reality. Maybe this is the learning ground for spiritual and personal growth.

"Don't let your mind control you.
Control your mind."

—Jocko Willink

Chapter 12

OVERCOMING THE SILENT BEAST

THEY SAY MARCH comes in like a lion and out like a lamb. That would be pretty descriptive of 2020 and 2021. Here came COVID. The atmosphere in New York State was to stay home and, if possible, work from there. Shield yourself from the world of disease.

Upper management was stunned and concerned about the future of the business. We had to apply to the Governor of New York to be considered an essential business, meaning that we could maintain our current status and continue to do business with some precautions in place.

Home improvement companies, which was the category we were listed under, were still assisting consumers with issues concerning their homes. With so many people now in their homes for long periods of time, home improvement and repair spending in the US grew by three percent. Consumers were interested in modifying living spaces for work, schooling, and leisure.

At the start of the pandemic, there were five of us in a room, trying to figure out the future steps for the business. Collectively, we reviewed the application, filled it out with all the details and facts we felt were imperative, sent it to the office of the governor, and anxiously waited for their response and approval.

Surprisingly, the response came back within twenty-four hours, and it deemed RBA of Western New York essential, and that was the best news. Business as usual, with a few minor changes. Safety for consumers and employees was the utmost important factor. With lockdowns and people getting sick, this was a difficult time, and it was difficult to maneuver around COVID cases and customer concerns. Working with a skeleton crew and handling the day-to-day was difficult and stressful. Each day introduced new problems and situations that demanded creative thinking. For example, how do you measure windows and doors and give estimates for someone's home when you're not allowed in the house?

The safety of my employees was at the top of my mind, along with the ability to respond to consumer demands and needs. Describing this time as a treadmill that didn't possess a kill button would be putting it lightly. When I was faced with decisions that would impact the business and its employees, I had to stay open-minded and understand that there was no other option but to monitor performance and numbers and build off of the positive at all times. I was always reinforcing the importance of a solid culture among all the departments and employees. The "victim" mentality needed to go away. I knew that I had to shed that feeling.

I feel, in many ways, I have already faced the "victim mentality" in my personal life. Having breast cancer and losing my soul mate took a toll on me. This is a very dark mindset to enter, and it is difficult to get out of. The victim mentality will bind your thoughts and stop you from clearly seeing the purpose of life. Let's face it; it is definitely an easier road to travel, but it is harmful, and it directly affects every part of your being. If you allow these types of defeating thoughts to take over, your landslide will be endless and unforgiving. I didn't want to live like that. I needed to pursue the other side. Feeling defeated in many ways, the internal struggle to pull myself out of this mindset was relentless. I don't think I've ever talked to myself as much as I have in the past year—it was exhausting. I read as much as I could, and I decided to post positive quotes on Facebook once a day that I felt would help others. These messages were also reminders for me. Alone time was essential, and although lonely, it was enlightening in many ways. Your coping mechanism comes into play, and you realize this is totally up to you, sink or swim. I needed to tap into all of my wonderful memories and past experiences. They have an important role in the process of moving on in a constructive and healthy manner.

As the year 2020 progressed, restrictions lightened slightly, employees were brought back to work, and it was full steam ahead. You would have thought it would have been a disastrous year, but on the contrary, it was another double-digit year for growth. My main objective was to find people who were willing and able to work and wanted to learn, grow, and become part of an organization with tremendous growth and opportunity. It seemed that finding people who took pride in their work was more difficult. The marketplace had changed, as it had for many industries. The reluctance to work or get back to work was prevalent. During many episodes of concern, I regularly found my thoughts gravitating toward the question: what would Don do? I needed to tap into all my experiences and all that I had been taught. Hopefully, I could utilize the information and education I'd accumulated over the years and react with the right steps to keep moving the business forward. I reflected on memories from time to time to put things into perspective. This helped me put an element of confidence back into my life that had disappeared when Don passed away. He was so patient and decisive, traits I admired.

As 2020 wrapped up, the tremendous growth, new employees, and new installation crews were flowing as they were designed to. Being part of the RBA Family, as I have expressed before, was like no other organization that I have witnessed or have been part of. Corporate was constantly sharing product information, continued education, and training. You name it—it was available to help you grow and improve your organization. RBA corporate also encouraged community involvement, showing support for those in need. To be in a position to give to others who are less fortunate offers a different perspective and personal satisfaction.

This was not a foreign idea to Don and me. Since our health club days, we always did what we could to support not only the local community but also other organizations like St. Jude's Children's Hospital. As our business grew, our donations followed suit. RBA corporate's mindset had always been to give back to the community, which meant so much to Don and me. I wanted to continue that after Don's passing, and when I reviewed what we would support with my team in 2020, we decided to support multiple facilities and organizations and one special individual. Our list consisted of Breast Cancer, St. Jude's Children's Hospital, Pirates Toy Fund, Roc Recovery, Education for Success, Story of Hope, and Mr. Denny Wright, a police officer who was wounded and blinded in the line of duty.

Every year, corporate RBA holds a summit for all the company-owned stores and affiliates. This function has grown tremendously in the years I have been involved. Due to 2020 COVID restrictions and concerns, it was announced that they were going to attempt to reproduce this function as if we were all there in person, but in actuality, everyone would be participating from their individual home states and offices.

As the date for the summit approached, I was notified that RBA of West New York was one of the contenders for the 2020 Community Award. I was excited on two fronts: being a contender for the community award, and if we were the winner, I could speak from the comfort of my own office and not have to walk on stage in front of hundreds of people. When the winner was announced, and we won the Community Award for 2020, the excitement from my team members and employees was enough for any leader to step back and take pride in all that we had accomplished together during the last couple of years. What a blessing. This was a great ending to a great year.

While sitting alone, going over the events of the day, the month, and the year, I was drawn into a vacuum of thoughts. I realized that this internal chatter was something I had come to terms with. Quieting the mind was still an obstacle for me, and I often questioned if I would ever be back in control. Maybe the control I so desired over my constant thoughts wasn't actually required or beneficial; maybe the control I wanted was only meant to assist me in detaching from everything. I realized I no longer wanted to be detached, and I had found purpose in my work.

Working alongside my team was inspirational and demanding. It was essential to attend all meetings and to fully understand all the logistics of the flow of the business. I was still learning the nuances of the business and understanding the differences between employees. Involving myself in everything was my choice because I wanted to learn and absorb as much as I could. The residual effect of COVID caused material shortages. Extended times for receiving products now demanded extended install dates, and the pipeline was growing.

By the time 2021 was upon us, I felt stronger and more confident in solving the daily issues. I strongly advised my management teams to keep their eyes on the target and protect culture at all times. Budget numbers reflected continuous double-digit growth, and this was demanding. My biggest fear was burnout, not for myself but for my employees. I wanted to make sure that each department was staffed so that this would not occur. Finding the "right" people to share in our culture and growth was a challenge. Space was also becoming an issue. Fortunately, these are all good things to have to worry about.

As the year edged to an end and our 2021 budgets were submitted to corporate, it was evident that this opportunity was never-ending, growing double-digits every year. I expressed to my management team, "Hold on. Here we go for another tremendous year." The teams worked well together and respected each other's input, and they seemed to be conscious of their common goals and how to go about achieving them. We penetrated the marketplace; we were a force to be dealt with on every level. Our accomplishment of hitting our milestones was recognized, and now we had to set new ones.

Running a business that was tracking numbers that had never been realized before in this region took a lot of focus and left me drained most nights. I often felt that work was like Groundhog Day. Growing pains became a steady flow in every department, but if you consider the alternative, everything was going in the right direction. Resolve, remain calm, research, and then initiate the required changes. Keep the train on the tracks. Keep moving forward. These were my mantras.

As another year came to an end, we prepared for another summit. Due to concerns about large group gatherings, it was canceled at the last minute and moved to Zoom. Although disappointing, I understood the reason for the cancellation. This year had gone by faster than the previous, and I was looking forward to seeing and connecting with others from corporate and the other affiliates.

A few weeks passed, and as I returned to the office after grabbing coffee, I entered the showroom and froze. I realized the entire company and my family were standing there waiting for me. Shocked would be putting it lightly. What the hell was going on?

As I was guided to the front of the showroom, I noticed the Vice President of Renewal by Andersen Corporate, Jeanne Junker, was on the large screen. She proceeded to inform me that she was extremely touched by my staff's input when they were asked to share their thoughts about me and my accomplishments. Jeanne, whom I'd always admired and looked up to, then announced that she presented a very special award every year, The Crystal Achievement Award for performance and perseverance, and that I was this year's winner. I felt like I had exited my body. I didn't realize my efforts and accomplishments were being noticed and acknowledged. I just assumed I was doing what needed to be done without exposing the struggles within. I felt eternally grateful for this acknowledgment, and this alone gave me the confidence to continue and open myself up to accepting the possibilities of more. To be recognized by those I looked up to and admired was amazing and humbling. I once again felt blessed on many levels, and I thanked God that I was not in front of everyone who would have been attending the summit.

After that, the professional side swung into high gear, but I felt the personal side dragged a little behind. When you're absorbed in the day-to-day tasks of running a business, there is little time to step back and reflect on your personal growth. Or, at least, I had convinced myself of that.

Work was occupying all of my time, so when my sister-in-law offered up a night out with the brothers, I jumped at the opportunity for a release. She purchased tickets to see a psychic in a group setting at a local restaurant and wine bar. This would be more like a family get-together, and I looked forward to changing it up. Since my mom had introduced this world to me at a young age by taking me to see psychics, I had no fear and was intrigued.

After Don's passing, I felt an impulse to sit with psychics to attempt to feel connected with my husband. I had a reading from a woman located in Liverpool who was recommended by a close friend. Keep in mind that this psychic knew nothing about me and didn't even have my name. This woman was undeniably the best psychic I had ever been to. The reading was filled with personal details about Don that only I would have been aware of. After the reading, I felt as if I had just spent the last hour with my husband. It was that clear and accurate. Although struck with loneliness, I was filled with hope and a desire to continue on my journey to learn everything I possibly could about this world. My faith propelled me forward to continue with the best outlook I could muster up.

The night of the event arrived. I had to go directly from work. The room, although not optimal for an event, was long and narrow, but they did offer complimentary wine, which was a nice touch. I was seated between my sister-in-law and a stranger, and the rest of my family was spread throughout the room. The door opened, and in walked an interesting-looking individual. Tall, thin, and wearing a black hat with a skeleton on it, he slowly moved through the crowd, introducing himself and explaining how he channels messages and delivers the information. He was confident, and I sensed impatience. I was intent on watching him closely. I was mesmerized, and I concentrated on what he was saying as he walked through the aisles.

As the evening continued, his messages seemed to hit home with many people. This medium definitely had a gift so few are blessed with. At one point in the evening, he shared a message with me from my mom, who was recently deceased, and it was spot on. This left me with a feeling of connectedness that was vital for my growth.

Psychics who are gifted are a blessing if you decide to connect with a loved one who has passed on. What is shared during a reading cannot be dismissed lightly. How can we attempt to explain this? And, maybe, we shouldn't have to. The messages are loving and comforting. What is the harm in that, to help guide someone through the stages of grief? It's been written for many centuries that the human body is what leaves the earth plane, and the spirit lives on for eternity and possesses the personality traits we always recognize as that person.

Communication from those who have passed comes in many different forms. Intuitive thoughts, dreams, visions, and direct messages, to name a few. Open yourself up to accepting all that surrounds you. Proof is in your acceptance of this knowledge, not ignorance.

This is our chosen journey. I repeat: *chosen*. The way it goes is entirely up to each of us. Carl Jung said it well:

"You are not what happened to you; you are what you choose to become."

After experiencing what I experienced the night my husband passed, I was unable to get the vision out of my head. My curiosity was piqued, and I was determined to try to find out more. This new curiosity influenced my reading habits, and I have read a lot of information on grief and spirituality. I came across this passage by an unknown author:

> "The death of a spouse or partner is different than other losses in the sense that it literally changes every single thing in your world going forward. The way you eat, the way you watch TV, your friend choice or friend circle dissolves, your family dynamic/life changes. Your financial situation, your job, your self-esteem, your confidence changes. Your rhythms, your mental and brain functions, your sense of humor, sense of womanhood or manhood changes. Your sense of security and your physical body, your hobbies change, every single thing changes. You are handed a new life that you never asked for and that you don't particularly want. It is the hardest, most gut-wrenching, horrific, life-altering of things to live with."

In my mind's eye, this is not the end; this is just one chapter of many to come. I cannot comprehend that there is life, and then there is death, and that's it. I believe there is so much more, and yes, it involves all of our emotions and thoughts. Without our beliefs, our hopes, and our faith, we are no different from those who exercise no growth or compassion, stifled in their minds by the idea that this is it.

We are touched by so many as part of our journey. Notice them; they are truly the small miracles of life. Grasp the idea of continuing for a bigger purpose. Grief is a messed-up cluster of emotions. Attempt to accept this and utilize this as an opportunity to become more present with yourself and others. It's an awakening to view reality from a different perspective. Search for your reason; be curious about your why. Live your truth, be grateful, be hopeful, and enjoy all that is to be enjoyed. Love those who love you and those who don't.

Grief is the silent beast we all must overcome!

About the Author

PATRICIA ANN is a driven and accomplished leader. She is the current owner of Renewal by Andersen of Western New York, a thriving home improvement company with a remarkable revenue and over one hundred dedicated employees. Prior to this, Patricia spent over a decade as the owner of a health club, which boasted a robust schedule of forty classes per week and employed forty staff members. Her professional journey has been defined by the strong belief that changing one's perspective is pivotal to changing the world, and she lives by the mantra that every day presents a new opportunity for transformation.

Patricia's commitment to fostering a culture that reflects the values of her own family has been a cornerstone of her career. She emphasizes the importance of family and personal growth. Her dedication and leadership have not gone unnoticed, as she has been nationally recognized by Renewal by Andersen, receiving the prestigious Crystal Achievement Award and the Community Award for her unwavering commitment to creating a better tomorrow.

Born into a family of five siblings, Patricia was raised believing that everyone is equal and that healthy competition is beneficial. Her journey and passion are deeply rooted in these values, and she continues to inspire those around her with her relentless drive and dedication to excellence.